A cast of thousands, all with important jo

Bricklayers build walls using bricks and cement.

Carpenters work on all the wooden parts of the buildings, including floors, doors, baseboards and staircases. They also make molds for concrete – this is called formwork.

Caterers provide food and drink for all those working on the building site.

Computer engineers and technicians design and install the airport computers.

Demolition workers knock down and remove old buildings from the new site. They drive and operate the bulldozers, scrapers and metal wrecking balls.

Environmental advisors assess how much disturbance a new airport might cause to local people and wildlife and offer advice on how to keep it to a minimum.

Electricians install and repair all the electrical equipment. They also install electrical wiring in the new buildings, for lighting and heating.

Plumbers install all the pipes which carry water around the buildings. They install the toilets and sinks, and the sprinkler systems which are needed in case of fire.

Scaffolders put up the scaffolding needed for the building work.

Surveyors and engineers study the suggested site for a new building or road. They test the rock and soil, to make sure that it is safe to build. Surveyors measure out the new building site. They use equipment such as theodolites and levels to help them mark out where everything will go.

Construction workers carry out the building work. They drive and operate many different machines – augers, excavators, paving machines, dump trucks, graders, rollers, pile drivers, scrapers, tunnelling machines and tower cranes.

Decorators put the finishing touches to the buildings. They hang the wallpaper, and paint the walls, ceilings and woodwork.

Glassworkers put glass in the windows and doors.

Heating specialists work with the plumbers and electricians to install the central heating systems.

Plasterers spread plaster over the walls before they are painted or wallpapered. Plaster is a soft paste that hardens when it dries.

Tilers lay all the tiles needed in the kitchens and wash rooms.

Welders join the ends of metal beams together using electrical arc welding sets.

Yardmen help to direct heavy machinery and vehicles all over the building site.

More than 15,000 people are needed to build an airport!

Let's Build an Airport

Contents

The airport is scheduled to take three years to build, that's just 36 months! The Project Engineer has made a Gantt chart so he can make sure everything runs smoothly. It shows how long each stage takes, when each job starts and when it must finish. It also shows which jobs can go on at the same time and which ones need to be finished before another one starts. The airport is finally finished almost 6 months late!

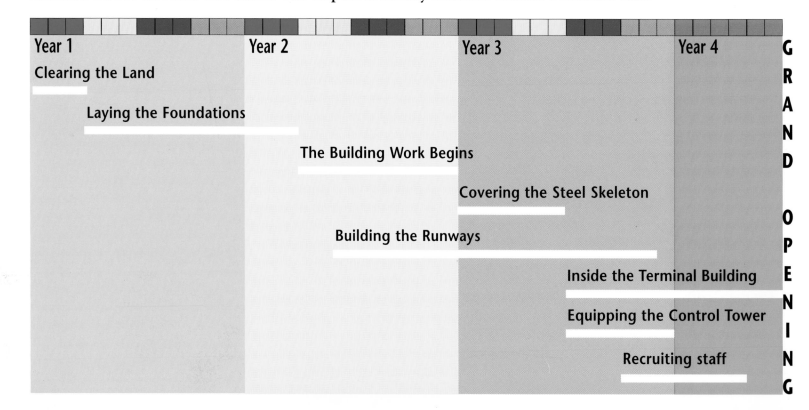

Year 1 | Year 2 | Year 3 | Year 4

Clearing the Land

Laying the Foundations

The Building Work Begins

Covering the Steel Skeleton

Building the Runways

Inside the Terminal Building

Equipping the Control Tower

Recruiting staff

GRAND OPENING

Copyright © 1998 Zero to Ten Ltd • Text copyright © 1998 Kath Mellentin • Illustrations copyright © 1998 Gillian Clements • Publisher: Anna McQuinn, Art Director: Tim Foster, Art Editor: Sarah Godwin, Designer: Tiffany Leeson • First published in the United States in 1998 by Zero to Ten Ltd, 95 Madison Ave, New York, NY 10016 • All rights reserved • No part of the publication may be reproduced or utilized in any form or by any means, electronic or mechanical, including photocopying, recording or by any information retrieval system, without the prior written permission of the Publisher • Library of Congress Catalog Card Number applied for • ISBN 1-84089-026-6 • Printed in Hong Kong

Written by Kath Mellentin   Illustrated by Gillian Clements

Consultants: Civil Engineer, Gareth Williams and First Officer, Mel Joyce

The site for a new airport is chosen very carefully. Many years of planning and discussion take place, involving thousands of people. Here are just a few of those involved…

Local residents and local government need to know how an airport will affect their lives. Will there be more noise and air pollution? Will a new airport be good for the area, bringing new jobs? Many people want to protect the wildlife on the proposed site.

A Public Hearing is held to discuss the issues. Anyone who feels the airport should not be built, or that the plans should be changed can go along to the meetings. The Chairperson of the Committee in charge of the Hearing can ask for reports from experts on different areas: noise, traffic, the environment, employment, the community…

When everything has been discussed, the Committee makes a decision and, if the decision is "yes", permission to go ahead is given.

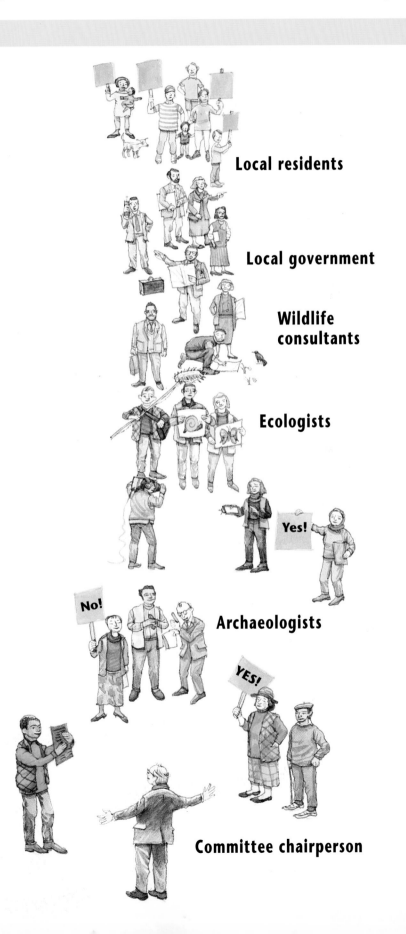

Local residents

Local government

Wildlife consultants

Ecologists

Yes!

No!

Archaeologists

YES!

Committee chairperson

This is the site for the brand new airport. There is lots of room for all the buildings and runways, and the engineers and surveyors who studied the site say that the land is flat and firm enough to build on.

Peter Child, the Environmental Advisor, and his team are finishing their work to make sure that the least possible damage is done to widlife and the environment. Now, Leon Howard, the Safety Officer, must ensure that the site is safe for the construction work to begin.

Every airport has similar runways, hangers and control towers. What gives an airport its own special feel is the terminal building. Sara Zadow, the Architect has come up with some wonderful light and airy designs for this new airport. The Airport Authority is very excited about them and can't wait until everything is complete.

Today the team of key people are coming to the site. They've had lots of meetings to plan everything, but this is the day that work really begins...

It will take more than three years to turn this empty patch of land into a working airport.

Alex, the Project Engineer, will work with Eric, the General Site Superintendant, to direct the building work. Between them, they must make sure that everything happens on time.

The Work Begins

Sara has to think about what building materials to use, and how to heat and light the buildings.

Before the building work begins, powerful bulldozers and scrapers clear and flatten the ground. The huge steel blades at the front of the bulldozers push great mounds of dirt and rubble out of the way, while the scrapers take off the top layers of earth.

Where the land has been cleared Tom Rodgers, the Civil Engineer, and his team "set out" the buildings. Together with the surveyors, they measure the site. They have detailed plans from the Architect and they put markers in the ground to show where the buildings will go. They use theodolites to position the markers.

There are strict safety rules on every building site. The Safety Officer must make sure everyone follows these rules.

Look out!

This spiked arm at the back of the bulldozer is called a ripper. It is used to break up rocks.

Clearing the Land

These old buildings are being demolished to make room for the airport fire station. A huge metal wrecking ball is swung against the walls to smash them down.

To help set out the ground for huge buildings, surveyors sometimes use GPS surveying equipment (which uses measurements to satellites in space) to mark important points on the ground.

Yum!

At last, work can begin on the airport terminal building. First of all foundations must be laid below ground. The rest of the terminal will be built on top of this firm base.

3

A tower crane uses a tool called an auger to drill deep holes in the ground. The auger twists down into the earth and rock like a giant corkscrew. Then concrete is poured into the holes. When it sets, the concrete will harden into long columns, called piles.

BANG! BANG! BANG! On another part of the site, a crane drops an enormous weight, called a pile hammer, down onto ready-made concrete piles, pushing them into the ground.

The pile foundations reach down into the firmer rock below. They will stop the terminal building from sinking under its own weight, or from slipping sideways.

What?

The workers must wear ear defenders to protect their ears from the deafening noise of the machines!

Laying the Foundations

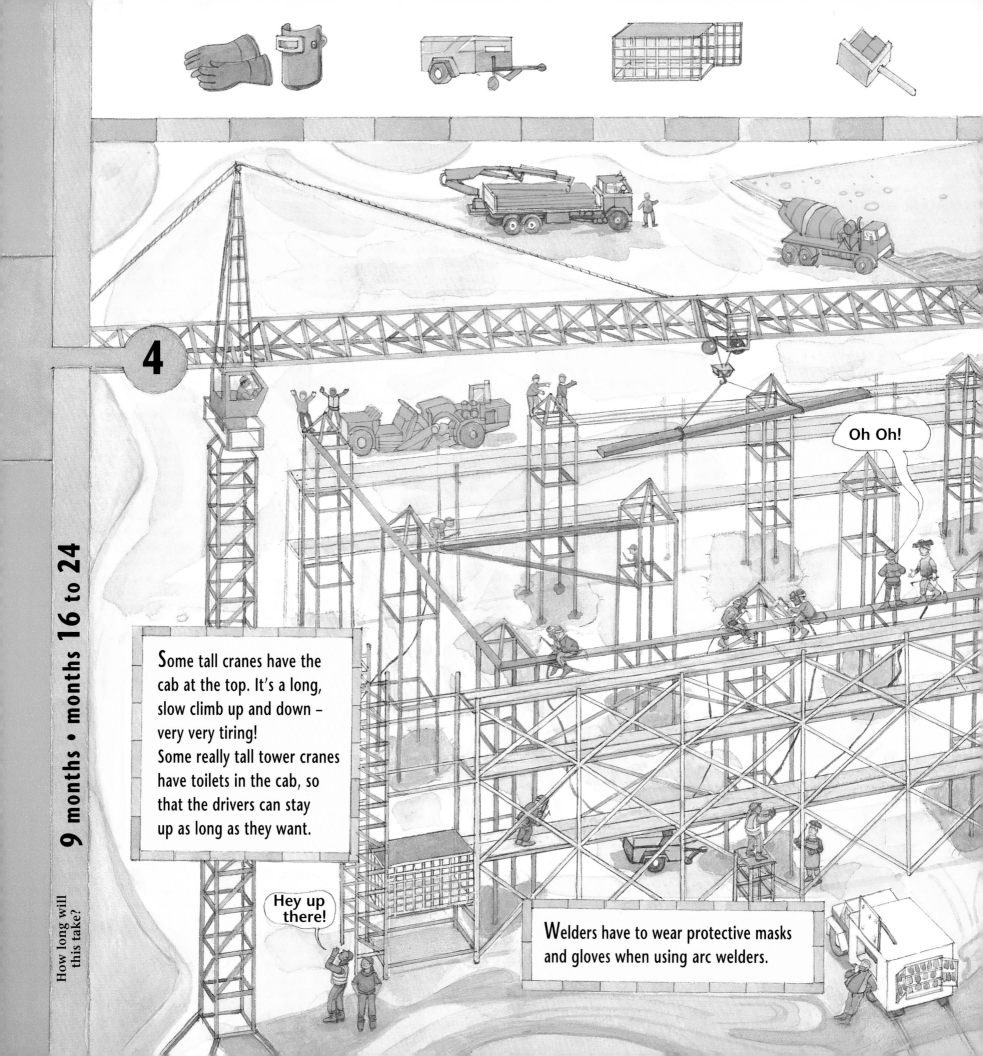

4

Oh Oh!

Some tall cranes have the cab at the top. It's a long, slow climb up and down – very very tiring!
Some really tall tower cranes have toilets in the cab, so that the drivers can stay up as long as they want.

Hey up there!

Welders have to wear protective masks and gloves when using arc welders.

The Building Work Begins

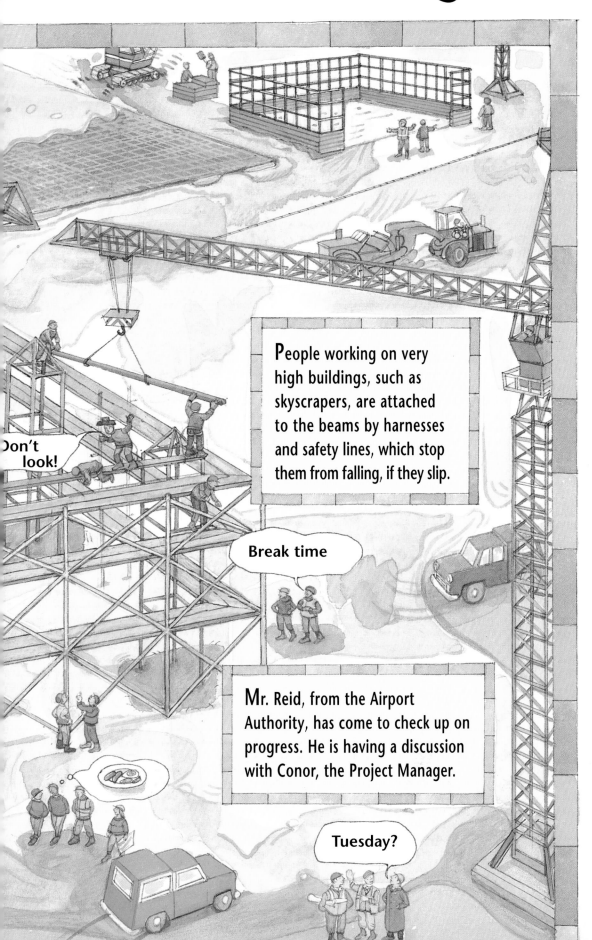

People working on very high buildings, such as skyscrapers, are attached to the beams by harnesses and safety lines, which stop them from falling, if they slip.

Don't look!

Break time

Mr. Reid, from the Airport Authority, has come to check up on progress. He is having a discussion with Conor, the Project Manager.

Tuesday?

The Architect, Sara, decided that the best way to design a bright, airy terminal building would be to use lots of glass panels supported by a strong steel frame.

Now the frame begins to take shape. Slowly, and with great care, gigantic cranes maneuver huge steel beams into place. The frame is like an enormous steel skeleton. It will give the terminal building its shape, and prop it up.

"Ooooh! Don't look down!" warns John, one of the welders, perched on the frame high above the ground. It is his job to join the steel beams. He uses an arc welder to join the beam ends together. Other workers use big nuts and bolts to attach cross braces to stiffen the frame. They push the bolts through holes, then tighten the nuts to fix them in place.

There's lots happening all over the site: work is underway on the runways and the frame of the terminal building is almost finished. Eric is relieved – all of the glass panels were delivered last Thursday! He watches as a tower crane carefully lowers the panels into place: they cover the frame like a skin and are held in place by bolts and clips.

"Easy does it!" cries Tony, the crane driver, from high in his cab, as a huge panel swings on the end of the jib.

5

In the meantime,

work continues far below on a tunnel for the underground railway. Like a gigantic drill, the tunnelling machine grinds through the earth and rock, turning it to rubble.

The control tower will be 150 feet tall, but it will be built in just three days. A steel mold is filled with concrete. Then, as the concrete sets, the mold is lifted up and the next layer poured in.

The workers often paint faces on the front of the tunnelling machine, and give it a name.

Covering the Steel Skeleton

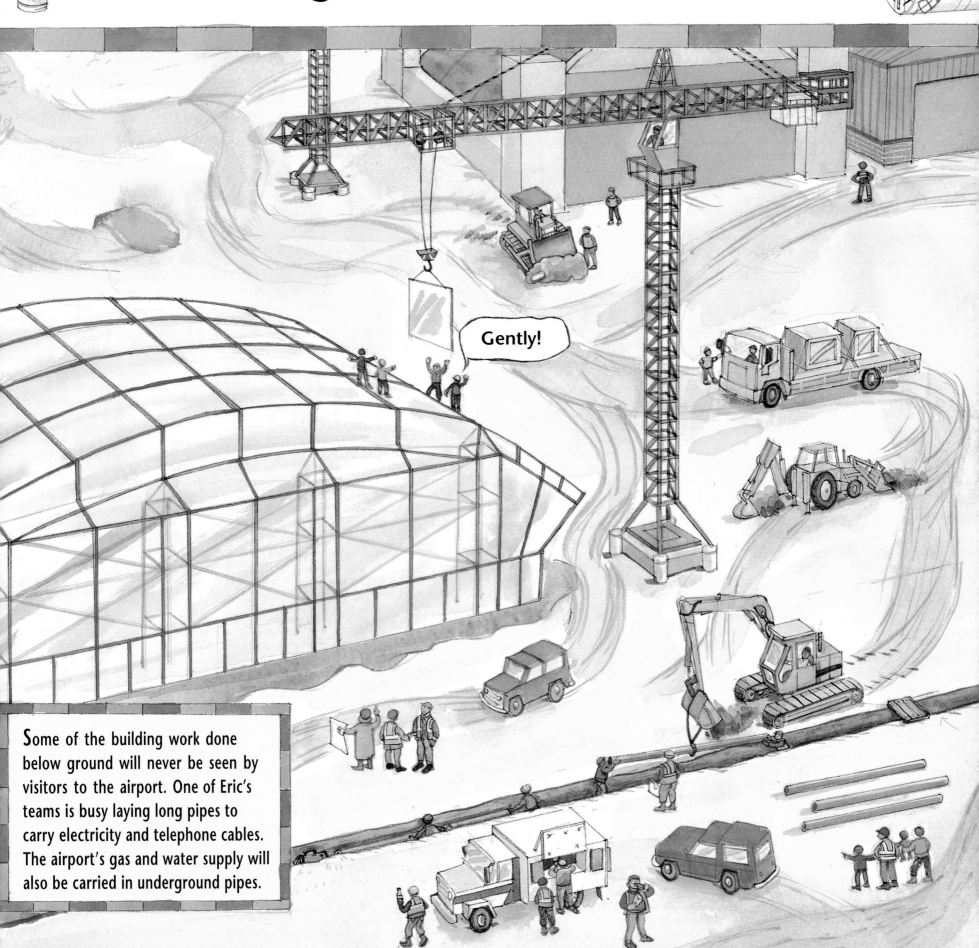

Some of the building work done below ground will never be seen by visitors to the airport. One of Eric's teams is busy laying long pipes to carry electricity and telephone cables. The airport's gas and water supply will also be carried in underground pipes.

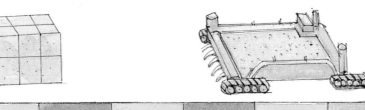

Eric checks his schedule and sighs: the tunnelling is ahead of time but the team of surveyors is over a week late. "At least work on the runways is really progressing quickly now," he thinks.

6 **A massive excavator** scoops out the soft, upper layers of earth, and loads the mounds of spoil into enormous dump trucks.

"Back a bit... STOP!" directs a yardman, shouting above the roaring engines. The trucks dump their loads at the edge of the building site.

A convoy of trucks arrives, carrying thousands of tons of stone to place along the runways. Graders spread the stone evenly with their wide blades, and then heavy rollers press it down firmly. A paving machine will form a thick concrete slab on top of the stone.

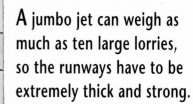

A jumbo jet can weigh as much as ten large lorries, so the runways have to be extremely thick and strong.

Building the Runways

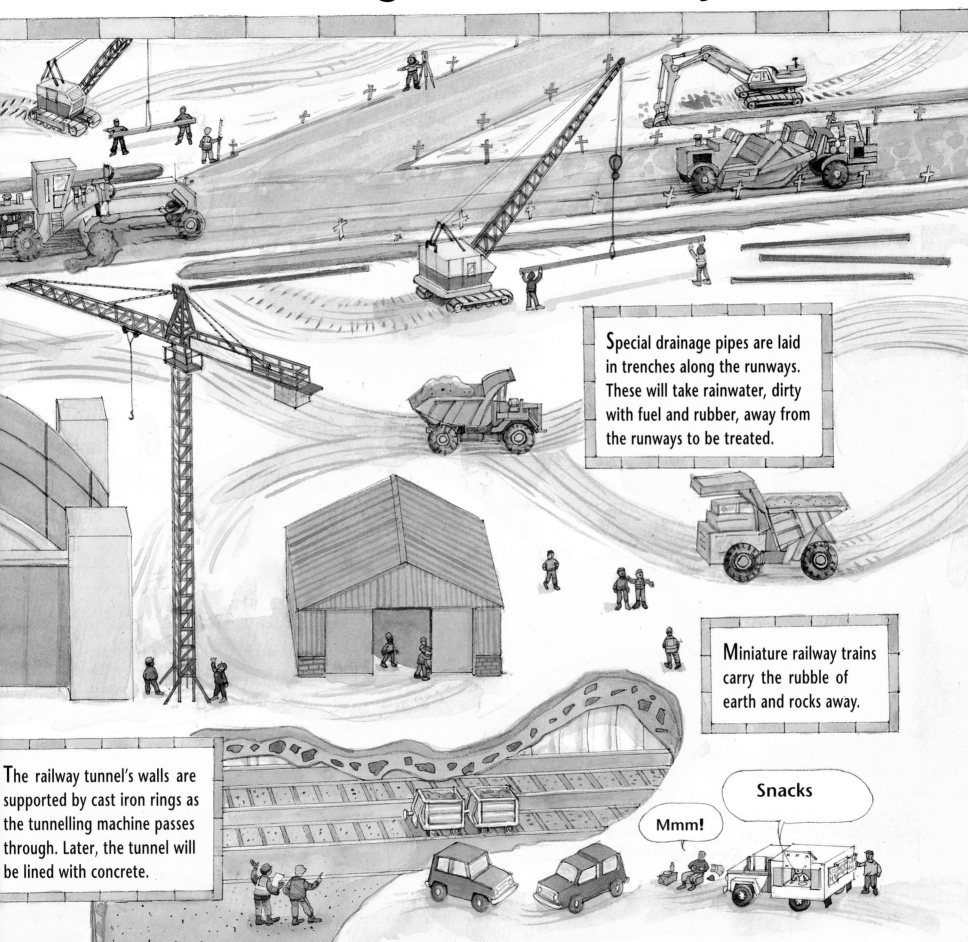

Special drainage pipes are laid in trenches along the runways. These will take rainwater, dirty with fuel and rubber, away from the runways to be treated.

Miniature railway trains carry the rubble of earth and rocks away.

The railway tunnel's walls are supported by cast iron rings as the tunnelling machine passes through. Later, the tunnel will be lined with concrete.

Snacks

Mmm!

Once the structure is complete, work can begin inside the terminal building. Teams of people, using many different skills, work together to get all the jobs done. Everyone is bustling around, and Leon, the Safety Officer, has to keep a strict eye out to make sure accidents don't happen.

Mandy Smith, an electrician, is doing the wiring in the departure lounge. She runs the wires under the floors and behind walls, where they cannot be seen.

Phil Gray, a carpenter, and his co-workers are busy putting up the store fronts. The walls and ceiling are lined with pieces of plasterboard.

7

"Watch out!" cries Leo Vezzani, one of the plumbers, as water spurts out of a leaking pipe, all over the freshly tiled floor.

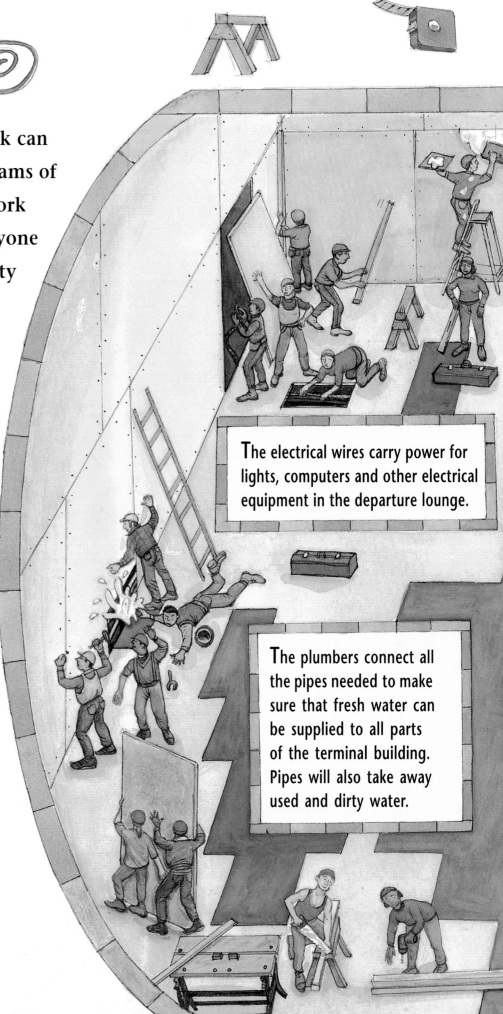

The electrical wires carry power for lights, computers and other electrical equipment in the departure lounge.

The plumbers connect all the pipes needed to make sure that fresh water can be supplied to all parts of the terminal building. Pipes will also take away used and dirty water.

Inside the Terminal

How long do they have left?

2 months

Only eight weeks to go, but the inside of the terminal is not yet finished. Everyone is working day and night to try to finish on time, but the long hours are making people tired, panicky and a bit on edge.

Alex has called a meeting to look at the schedule. With Eric, Rosa, Joe, Tom and Lian, he will try to deal with the last minute problems and get the project back on schedule. "Sometimes it's hard to believe that it will be ready in time!" sighs Tom.

The Carpet Layers are ready to lay the new carpet in the departure lounge... but they must wait while Mandy checks the wiring for the display screens. The team from "Sign-Rite" are putting up signs and notices. They look at the plans to check where the signs should go.

8

Finishing Touches

The metal detector will help to check if travellers are carrying anything dangerous.

Specially trained electrical engineers come to install the security equipment. The X-ray machines will be used to check what is inside everybody's bags without opening them.

It's not finished yet!

Wake up!

The seats for the departure lounge have just been delivered. But they can't be put in place until the carpets have been laid.

Over at the control tower things are hectic! Soon it is time to install the lights that mark out the runways in bad weather and at night.

The control tower is equipped with computer radar equipment which will guide the planes safely in and out of the airport.

Taro and Mike test the radio system which will be used by air traffic controllers to keep in close contact with the pilots. "Testing, testing...
Alpha Foxtrot Romeo Delta Charlie OVER." Everything works loud and clear.

9

A huge red and white radar dish is put up on the runway. It will send out invisible radio waves. When these waves meet a plane, they will bounce back to the dish. This will show up as dots of light on the radar screens in the control tower. This allows the air traffic controllers to keep track of exactly where all the planes are.

Some of the equipment is very delicate and must be handled with great care. Rosa has brought in a team of specially trained computer engineers to carry out this important work.

Air traffic controllers will guide the planes on the ground as well as in the air. The control tower is in the middle of the airport so that they have a good view over the whole airport.

Equipping the Control Tower

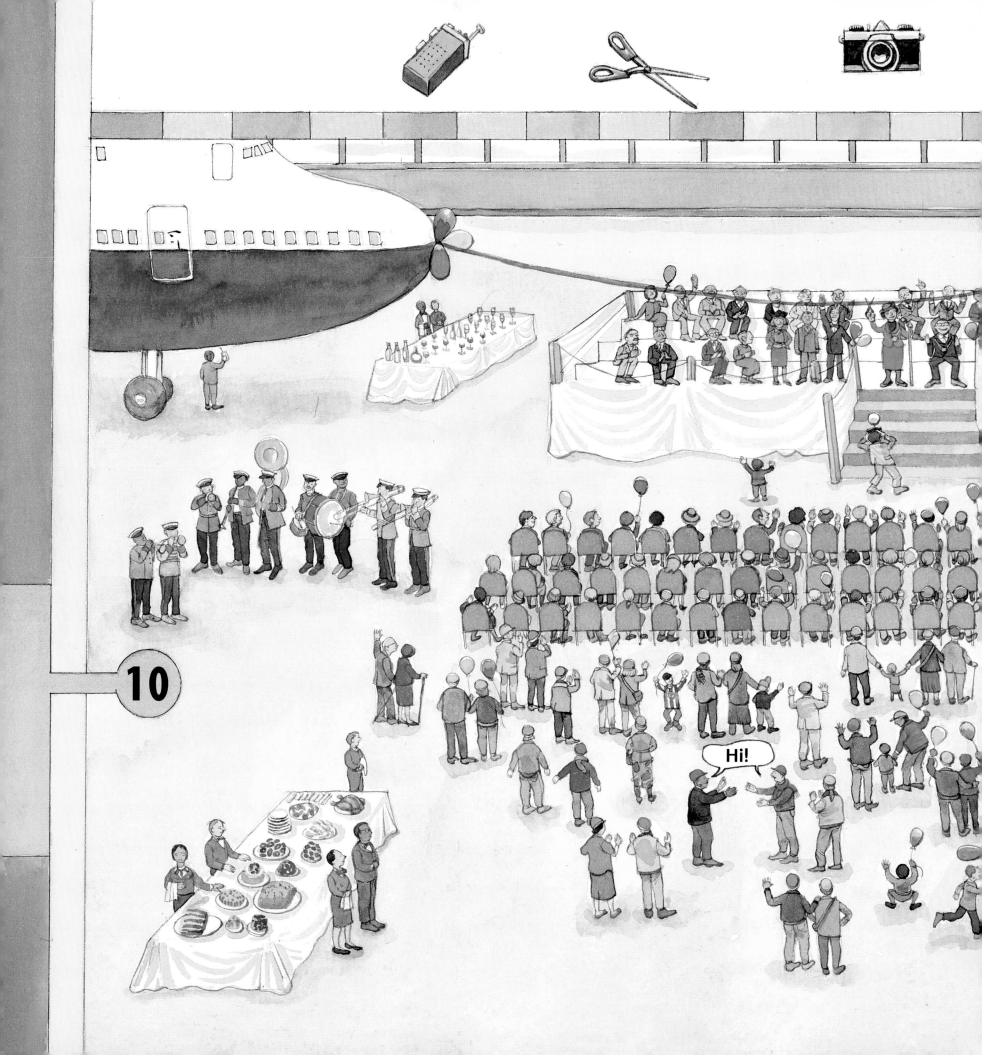

The Grand Opening

...open!

The paint is barely dry when the day of the grand opening ceremony arrives! All the important people from the Airport Authority are there, delighted that their airport is finally finished. Sara, Alex and Conor stand proudly on the platform with Mr. Reid.

A big crowd has gathered for the opening and all the workers are there as well as local people and reporters from the newspapers and television.

Mr. Reid holds up his hands for silence and the Mayor clears her throat. "Ladies and gentlemen," she announces, "I now pronounce this airport OPEN!" Then she snips the red ribbon to loud applause and flashing cameras.

Eric and his family watch from the crowd. "Well!" smiles Eric. "It was hard work, but we all did a good job – I think I could use a vacation now!"

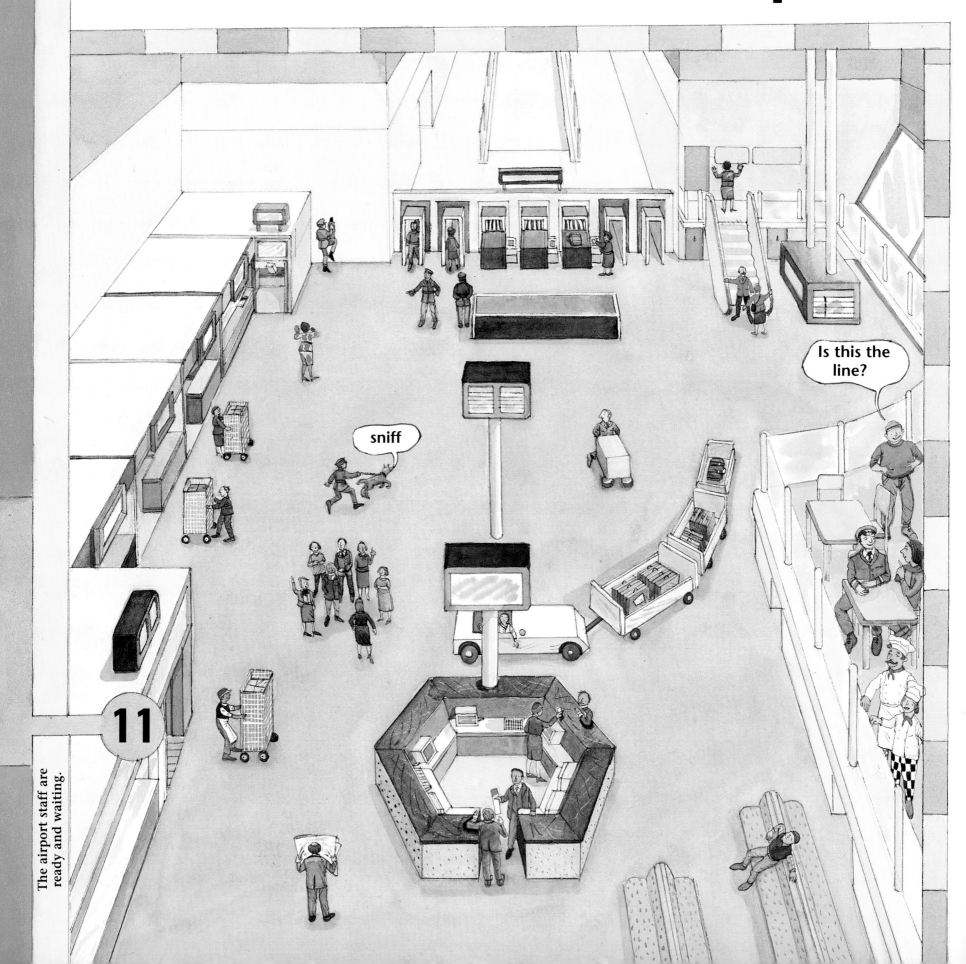

The airport staff are ready and waiting.

The duty manager is in charge of the day to day running of the whole airport.

Information assistants give out information to passengers.

Check-in agents welcome passengers at the check-in counters. They check tickets, hand out boarding cards and label luggage.

Baggage handlers load luggage off the planes and put them on the conveyor belts into the terminal building.

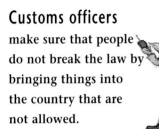

Customs officers make sure that people do not break the law by bringing things into the country that are not allowed.

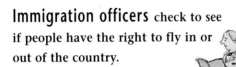

Immigration officers check to see if people have the right to fly in or out of the country.

Security staff scan passengers and luggage at the security gate to make sure that everything is in order

15,000 people were recruited to work in the airport! The airlines employ flight crew who work on the planes and ground staff who work in the airport. The Authority employs people to run the airport, and to work in the stores and cafes, to take care of cleaning, security, safety and so on – it's just like a small town.

The Captain and First Officer (the cockpit crew) fly the planes.

Red Caps are responsible for the planes. They check that the flight schedule, cargo, fuel, passengers and catering are in order and hand the final paperwork to the Captain to sign just before take-off.

Air traffic controllers work in the control tower, guiding planes in and out of the airport.

The cabin crew look after passengers while they are on board the plane and make sure they have a safe and pleasant flight.

Flight engineers look after the planes and refuel them after long flights.

Restaurant staff prepare food and serve it to people in the airport restaurants.

Store staff serve in the airport stores.

Cleaners keep the airport buildings spick and span.

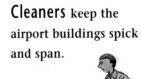

Fire officers are on hand night and day, to answer all sorts of emergency calls.

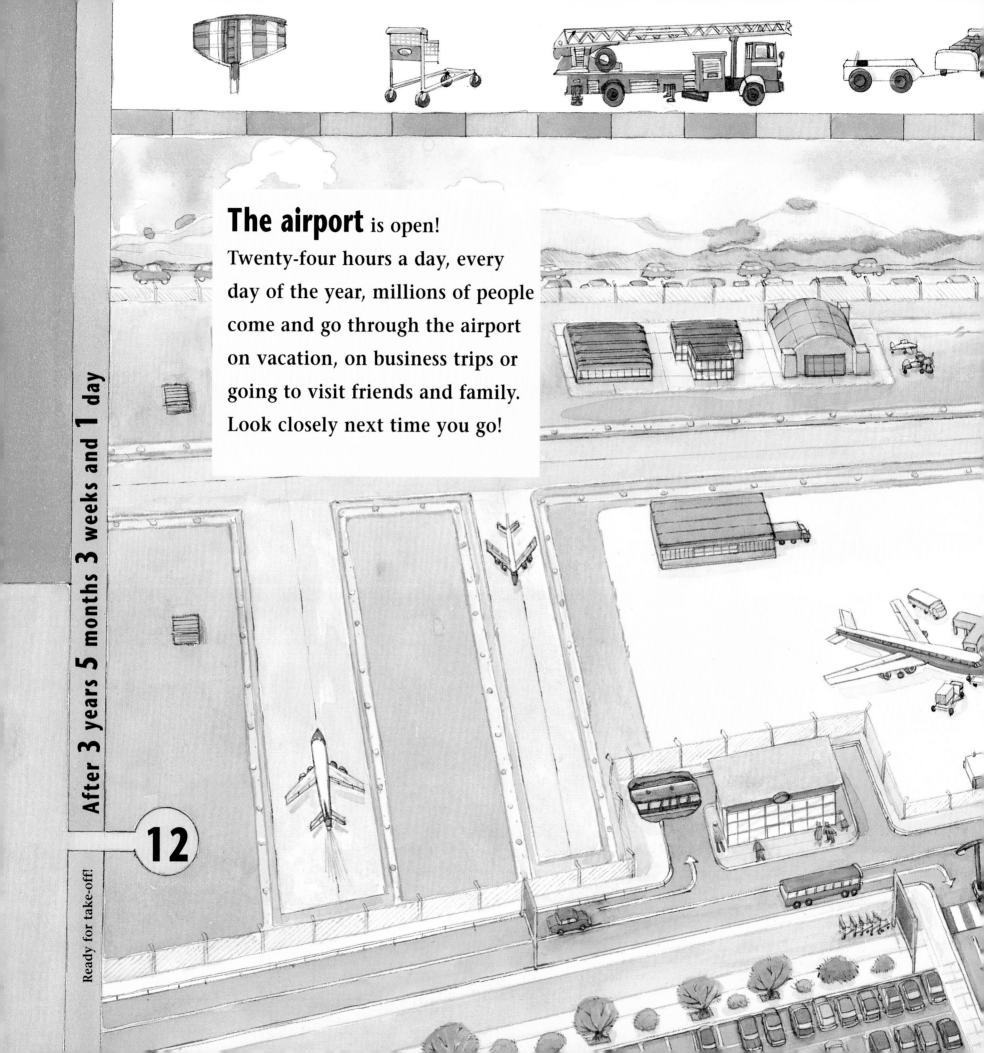

The airport is open! Twenty-four hours a day, every day of the year, millions of people come and go through the airport on vacation, on business trips or going to visit friends and family. Look closely next time you go!

12

The Airport at Work

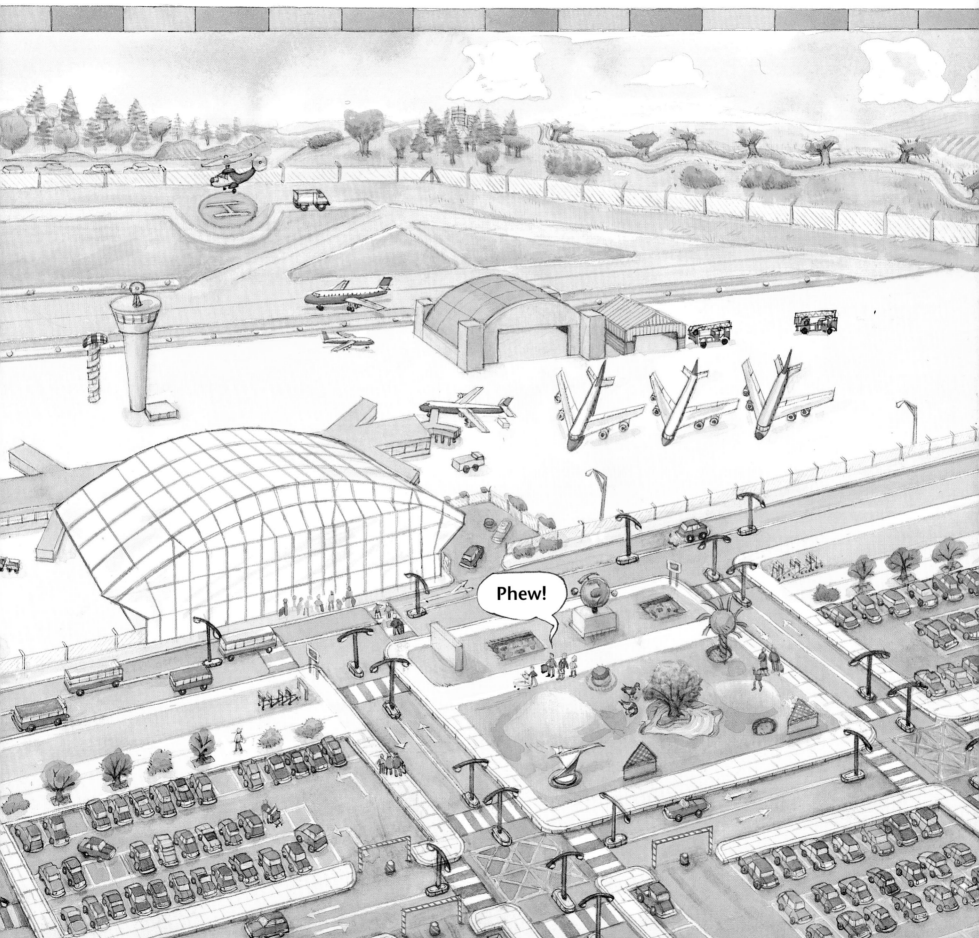

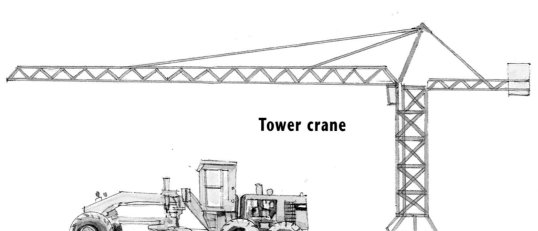

Tower crane

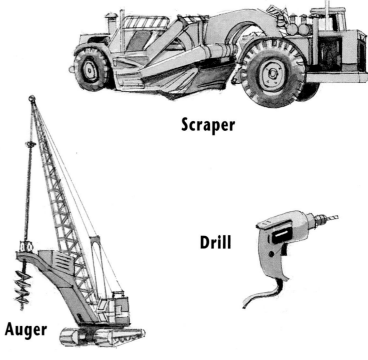

Scraper

Grader

Auger

Drill

Theodolite

Excavator

Tunnelling machine

Dump truck

GPS equipment

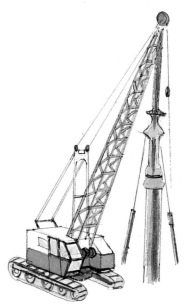

Bulldozer

Pile driver

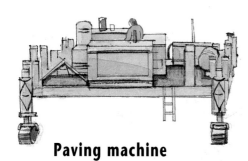

Paving machine

Plastering tool